CITIZENS
Who Made a Difference

by Carol Domblewski

W9-BPN-851

Table of Contents

Pictures To Think About i

Words To Think About iii

Introduction 2

Chapter 1 Mary McLeod Bethune 4

Chapter 2 Rachel Carson 10

Chapter 3 Cesar Chavez 16

Conclusion 21

Solve This Answers 22

Glossary 23

Index 24

Pictures To Think About

CESAR E. CHAVEZ

Words To Think About

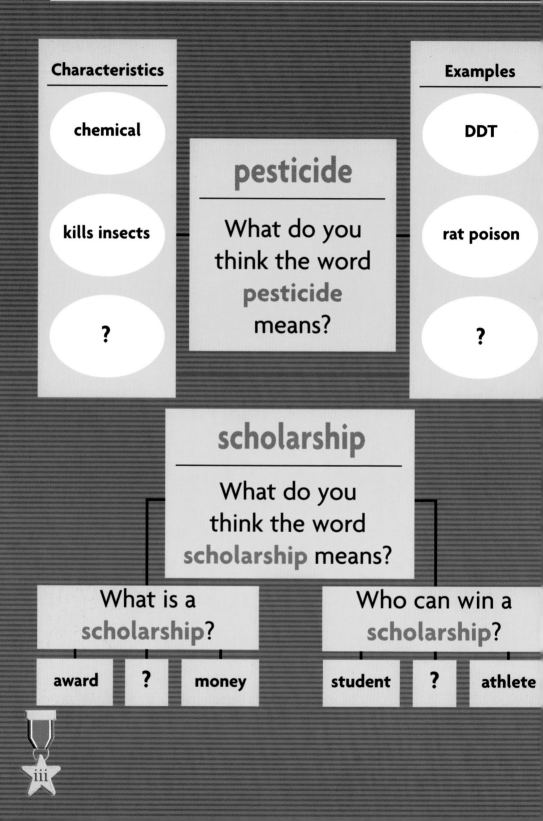

Characteristics

chemical

kills insects

?

pesticide

What do you think the word **pesticide** means?

Examples

DDT

rat poison

?

scholarship

What do you think the word **scholarship** means?

What is a **scholarship**?

award | ? | money

Who can win a **scholarship**?

student | ? | athlete

iii

Read for More Clues

pesticide,   page 12
scholarship,   page 5
strike,   page 19

strike

What do you think the word **strike** means in this book?

Meaning 1
to swing at a baseball and miss
(verb)

Meaning 2
to hit
(verb)

Meaning 3
when workers stop working
(noun)

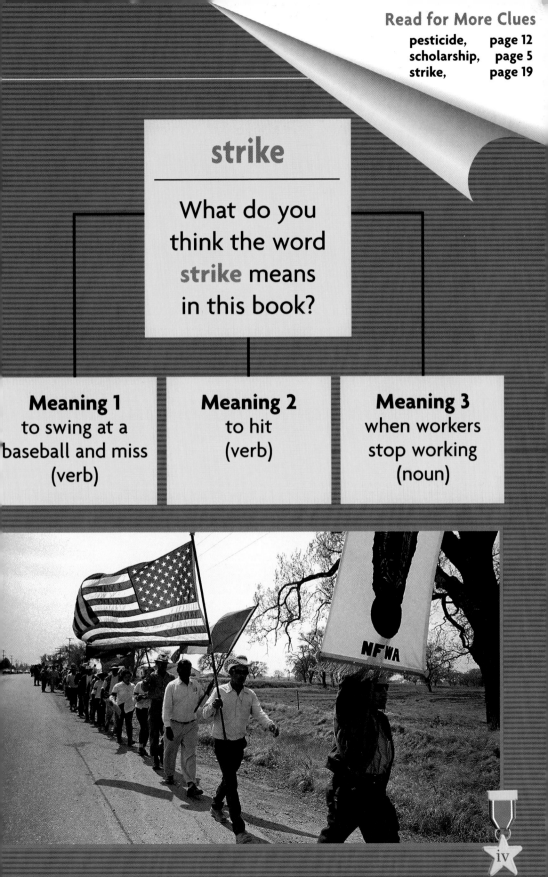

Introduction

In this book you will meet three people. Each one made the world a better place.

Mary McLeod Bethune saw that African American children could not go to school. She worked hard. She fought for the children's right to go to school.

Rachel Carson saw that some people were hurting Earth. These people were not keeping our air, water, and land clean and pure. She worked to protect Earth.

▲ Mary McLeod Bethune helped many children get a better education.

Cesar Chavez (SHAH-vez) saw the hard lives that farm workers led. Farm workers worked long days in the fields. They got low pay. He fought to get them a better life.

Read on to find out more about these great people. Learn why they are still important today.

▲
Rachel Carson helped save our natural world.

▲
Cesar Chavez fought to get farm workers better jobs and higher pay.

Mary McLeod Bethune

Hard Work, No School

Mary McLeod Bethune was born on July 10, 1875. She was born free. Her parents had been slaves. Her family had a small farm in South Carolina. Mary and her family worked in the fields every day. They grew cotton.

Mary's mother also did laundry for people. One day Mary went with her mother to bring back clean laundry. She saw a book. She picked up the book. Then a child grabbed the book away from her. The child said, "Put that down. You can't read." Mary knew then that she wanted to learn how to read and write.

MYTH OR REALITY?

It is said that Mary McLeod Bethune was born with her eyes wide open. Mary's mother was told that this was a gift. Her daughter would "see" things before they happened.

Mary Goes to School

Mary went to school when she was seven. Her school was only for African American children. Every day she walked five miles to school. Then she walked five miles home.

Mary went to this school for four years. Then she won a **scholarship** (SKAH-ler-ship). She won money to pay for her to keep going to school. She went to a school in North Carolina. She left home to go to this school. She was only twelve.

▲ This is the cabin where Mary McLeod Bethune was born.

1. Solve This

Write a number sentence that shows how many miles Mary walked every week. Base your sentence on a five-day week. The number sentence will give your answer as to how many miles she walked in a week.

Math✓ POINT:

How can you use multiplication to solve this problem?

5

Starting a School

Mary finished school. She wanted to be a teacher. There were few schools for African Americans. Mary started her own school.

In 1904, Bethune opened her school. The school was just for girls. It had only five students. She used every cent she had to start the school. Her desk was an old barrel. Some of the chairs were just old crates.

2. Solve This

Mary earned $2.00 toward the rent for her first school. The rent was $11.00. How much more did she have to earn?

Math ✓ POINT:

How can addition help you check your answer?

✓ POINT: Reread

Reread the second paragraph. Using the information, draw a picture of what you think the inside of Mary Bethune's first school looked like.

Something from Nothing

The school was a success. In two years it had 250 students. Bethune needed more space. She needed more land. She and the girls baked and sold pies. She bought land with the money they made. The land had been the city dump.

The girls at the school learned math and history. The girls also learned how to cook and sew.

◀ **Mary McLeod Bethune with her students**

3. Solve This

The land at the dump cost $250. Bethune earned $5.00 toward the cost by selling food. She owed $245.00 more. What symbol goes in the blank to make this expression true?

$250.00 __ $5.00 = $245.00

Math ✓ POINT:

How can addition help you check your answer?

Success

The school grew. First it was a high school. Then it became a college. By 1923, the school had 300 students. It had eight buildings. It even had a farm.

Mary McLeod Bethune spent twenty years building her school. It still stands today.

▲ Today, Bethune's school is a successful and popular college.

A Famous Citizen

Bethune did much more than start a school. She taught adults to read and write. She helped people vote. She gave advice to presidents of the United States.

Bethune was born poor. Still, her life was rich. She helped make the world a better place.

"I had faith in a living God, faith in myself, and a desire to serve."
—**Mary McLeod Bethune**

STAMP OF SUCCESS

How would you honor a hero like Mary McLeod Bethune? The United States Postal Service put her on a stamp.

▲ **Mary McLeod Bethune with President Harry Truman**

Mary McLeod Bethune

Black Heritage USA 22

9

Rachel Carson

The Beauty of Nature

Rachel Carson was born in 1907. Rachel's family lived on a farm. The farm was in Pennsylvania. Rachel loved to walk in the woods. She watched the fish in the streams. She listened to the songs of the birds. She loved nature.

Rachel's mother had a special seashell. Rachel would hold the shell to her ear. She thought she could hear the ocean. She had never seen the ocean. She knew she would see it one day.

young Rachel Carson ▶

A Young Writer

Rachel loved more than just nature. She also loved to write. At age eleven, she had her first story published in a magazine. She decided to study writing in school.

Her love of nature never left her, though. Rachel wanted to be a scientist, too. She studied biology, worked in a lab, and did research. Over time, she combined her two interests into one job. She became a famous nature writer.

Historical Perspective

Today women do many kinds of work. When Carson was born, not many women went to college. Very few women became scientists.

As a college student, ▶ Rachel Carson became interested in science.

A Deadly Danger

Carson wrote three famous books. The books were about the ocean. She wanted to keep writing about nature. Then she heard bad news. Wild birds were dying. **DDT** (dee-dee-TEE) seemed to be the cause. DDT is a **pesticide** (PES-tuh-side). Pesticides are chemicals. These chemicals kill insects.

DDT was not just killing insects. DDT was killing birds and other animals. Carson decided to study DDT. She wanted to know what DDT did to nature.

It's a Fact

Another word for *insecticide* is *pesticide.* Find the word *insect* insecticides. Insecticid kill insects. Find the word *pest* in *pesticide* Pesticides kill pests, including insects. Bot words contain the root *cide*. This root means "death."

▲ In the 1950s, farmers sprayed DDT on crops.

12

Silent Spring

Carson learned that DDT went into the **food chain**. A food chain is a group of living things that depend on one another for food. The first living thing is eaten by the second, and so on. Look at the drawing on this page. It shows how DDT reaches bigger animals, like humans.

In 1962, Carson published *Silent Spring*. Her book told how bad DDT was and how it hurt nature.

Carson said that DDT would kill all the birds. She wrote that we would have a spring without the sound of birds singing. She titled her book about DDT *Silent Spring*.

DDT Travels Through the Food Chain

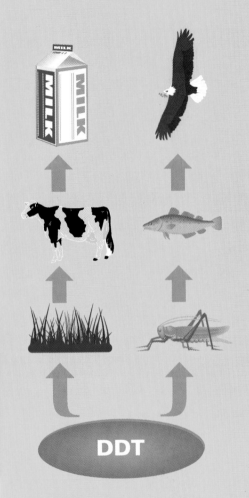

▲ The amount of DDT didn't stay the same as it went through the food chain. Larger animals took in more DDT than smaller insects and animals.

The Power of a Book

Many people read *Silent Spring*. Most people got mad. Would all the birds die? Maybe people would get sick and die, too!

The companies that made DDT said Carson was wrong.

▲ Rachel Carson being interviewed about her book

President John F. Kennedy asked a group to study what Carson had written. The group said she was right. In 1972, a new law stopped most uses of DDT.

☑ POINT:

Read More About It

To learn more about DDT, ask your teacher or librarian to help you find information in books or on the Internet.

Save Our Earth!

Rachel Carson made a difference. She showed people the truth. She showed people why they should take care of Earth.

Now we celebrate Earth Day. On this day, people clean up their towns and cities. People think about ways to keep Earth clean. They work to keep animals safe and healthy. They work to keep people safe and healthy, too.

STAMP OF SUCCESS

The United States honored Rachel Carson with this stamp. What would you add to the picture on this stamp?

MYTH OR REALITY?

Some people think DDT is all bad, but that's not true. Today millions of people in poorer countries die from malaria. Insects spread this serious disease. DDT is a cheap way to kill the insects and save those lives. DDT must be used very carefully, however.

Cesar Chavez

Working on the Farm

Cesar Chavez was born in 1927. Cesar lived on a ranch. The ranch was in Arizona. Then his family lost their ranch. Cesar was ten years old. His parents went to work on farms. His parents picked crops. They moved from place to place. They were **migrant workers** (MY-grunt WER-kerz).

It's a Fact

When they had jobs, migrant workers could live where they worked. But conditions were bad. Some places had no bathrooms. Some had no running water. Some had no electricity.

Migrant workers ▶ worked the fields picking crops.

Growing Up

The family had to work very hard. The family got very low pay. Sometimes they did not get paid at all.

The growers were not always fair. One time, the family was hired to pick cherries. The family was told they would get two cents per pound. The family began to work. Then the grower said he would just pay one cent per pound. The family needed money. They kept working.

4. Solve This

This table shows different rates of pay that Chavez's family earned in the fields.

Rate of Pay	Pounds Picked	Earnings
1 cent per pound	10	?
2 cents per pound	10	?
3 cents per pound	5	?

How much did the Chavez family make on each job?

▲ These migrant workers are cutting cabbage.

17

Farm Workers Unite!

Chavez wanted to help the farm workers. When Chavez grew up, he talked to the workers. He asked them to form a team. The team could fight for higher pay. The team could work for a better life.

5. Solve This

Look at the bar graph. In 1965, the lowest rate was 90 cents per hour. When the strike ended in 1970, many grape pickers got about $1.80 per hour for the low rate. Look at the low rate for 1965. How much more did a worker earn per hour in 1970 than in 1965 at the low rate?

Math ✓ POINT:

How might rounding up make it easier to solve the problem?

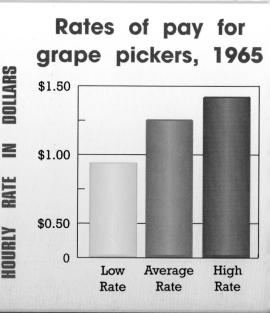

Rates of pay for grape pickers, 1965

HOURLY RATE IN DOLLARS

$1.50

$1.00

$0.50

0

| Low Rate | Average Rate | High Rate |

The Grape Strike

The workers formed a **union** (YOON-yun). A union is a group of workers. The union can ask for fair pay or safer ways to work. A union can also go on **strike**. A strike means workers stop working until their goals are met.

Chavez was the head of the union. In 1965, the union went on strike. The workers would not pick grapes. They would not work until their pay went up. Would the growers give in?

▲ Millions of Americans showed their support for the farm workers. To show support they **boycotted** (BOY-kaht-ed) grapes. This means they refused to buy grapes.

Success

In 1970, most grape growers gave in. They gave the farm workers more pay. They also gave them safer working conditions.

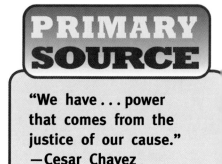

PRIMARY SOURCE

"We have . . . power that comes from the justice of our cause."
—Cesar Chavez

Chavez kept working for the farm workers. He helped pass the first law to help farm workers. He also spoke out against pesticides. These chemicals were sprayed on the fields. They killed the insects. They also hurt the farm workers. Chavez spent his life working for farm workers. He made a difference.

STAMP OF SUCCESS

The United States honored Cesar Chavez with this stamp. How would you honor Cesar Chavez?

USA 37

CESAR E. CHAVEZ

2003

Conclusion

Mary McLeod Bethune, Rachel Carson, and Cesar Chavez all changed the world. They had courage. They never gave up. As a result, the world is a better place.

| Mary McLeod Bethune | Rachel Carson | Cesar Chavez |
| better education | better environment | better working conditions and pay |

A Better World

Cesar Chavez liked to say, "Sí, se puede." Rachel Carson and Mary McLeod Bethune would have said the same thing: "It can be done!"

Solve This Answers

1 Page 5: 5 miles, 2 times a day: 5 + 5 = 10
10 miles a day, 5 days a week: 10 + 10 + 10 + 10 + 10 = 50
Math Checkpoint: If she walks 10 miles a day for 5 days, you can multiply 10 x 5 to get 50.

2 Page 6: $9.00
Math Checkpoint: You can reverse the problem, by taking the answer, which is 9, and adding 2, for this answer: 9 + 2 = 11

3 Page 7: − (a minus sign)
Math Checkpoint: You can reverse the problem, by taking the answer, which is $245, and adding $5, for this answer:
245 + 5 = 250.

4 Page 17: 10 cents; 20 cents; 15 cents

5 Page 18: $.90, or twice as much.
Math Checkpoint: $.90 rounds up to $1.00, and $1.80 rounds up to $2.00. $2.00 is twice as much as $1.00.